Dealing With Adversity:
10 Step To Thrive During Hard Times

Kenneth T. Hernandez

Table of contents

Chapter 1
Chapter 2
Chapter 3
Chapter 4
Chapter 5
Chapter 6
Chapter 7
Chapter 8
Chapter 9

Chapter 1

Find your sense of humor

A person's best quality may be their sense of humor.

This ability can help you communicate more effectively with people, enhance your health, and even defuse potentially explosive situations.

What's not frequently recognized is that having a sense of humor doesn't need to be humorous; all you need to do is learn to look at things from a different perspective.

recognizing humor

1 List the advantages of comedy.

You may discover humor in both happy and unhappy circumstances if you have a sense of humor.

A sense of humor may improve coping mechanisms and self-esteem while reducing stress and anxiety.

Humor has positive effects on the body, mind, emotions, and social interactions, such as easing pain and stress, boosting creativity and mood, making people friendlier, and improving interpersonal relationships.

2 Understand the distinction between humor and humility.

Being funny requires the ability to articulate humor, such as through the telling of a humorous narrative, a clever pun, or a well-timed joke.

Having a sense of humor is being able to laugh at—or at least find humor in—absurdities. life also implies being able to let go and not take things too seriously.

You don't have to be humorous or the one cracking jokes to have a sense of humor.

3 Find your sense of humor.

What causes you to smile?

What makes you laugh and feel lighter?

One method to start enhancing your sense of humor is by doing this.

There are many different kinds of humor, including joking around and laughing at life humor.

Watch and take notes.
Watch other individuals if you're unsure of how to laugh or find humor in situations.
How do your family and friends make light of their surroundings and their misfortunes?

Consider watching comedies starring Bill Murray, Eddie Murphy, Adam Sandler, Kristen Wiig, Steve Martin, or Chevy Chase, to name a few.
Watch comedy classics like Bridesmaids, Blazing Saddles, Trading Places, Monty Python and the Holy Grail, Young Frankenstein, Meet the Parents, and Young Frankenstein.
Be careful to observe others, but avoid simply mimicking their sense of humor.
True humor is sincere and reflects who you are.

5 Put more emphasis on enjoyment than humor.

Regardless of what life throws at you, having a sense of humor allows you to enjoy yourself.

That implies that you are free to make fun of yourself and life.

Keep your attention on having fun.

Understanding jokes

1. Pick up a few jokes.

Humor may be a terrific way to connect with others.

Learn some simple jokes if you wish to add some humor to social occasions.

Additionally, you can seek amusing images, clever quotes, and entertaining internet memes to share with others.

Search for items that fit your sense of humor.

Try something like this, for instance:

What do you name a group of bunnies moving backward in a line?

a hare line that's fading.

What was the broken vending machine's response to the football coach?
My quarterback, please!

2 Discover the humor in similarities.
Jokes about their circumstances, where they reside, or their views frequently draw laughter from the audience.
To ease the conversation, crack a light joke about the weather or the place you call home.
Make a joke about your line of work if you both work there.

Comment on the weather when you're trying to think of something to say.
For instance, "I'll have to ski to work if it doesn't stop snowing."

3 Spend time with humorous individuals.
Consider your humorous buddies.
How do they subtly insert humor into the dialogue?
What sort of jokes are they telling?

Watch stand-up comedians live or online videos. Pay attention to their delivery, the subjects they cover, and the way they inject humor into the banal.

Determine what it is about the individuals in your life that you find hilarious that you may include in your comedy by keeping an eye out for them.

4.Practice.

Jokes should be practiced to get better and seem more natural.

Begin by making jokes with dependable relatives and friends.

Describe your objective to them and request their frank cooperation.

If they advise you to make your jokes funnier, pay attention to what they say.

As you get more at ease, try extending it by adding comedy to chats with distant acquaintances.

5. Be mindful not to anger anyone.

As you refine your sense of humor, consider the situation.

Do you easily become offended by jokes made by others?

You should be careful not to offend or hurt anyone's feelings when speaking or laughing at jokes.

When you have a sense of humor, you have a positive outlook on life.

You shouldn't make fun of other people or exploit them as a way to make yourself laugh.

Consider the setting when cracking jokes.

Is this joke appropriate for a date, the office, or the group you're with?

Will it make someone angry?

Understand the distinction between punching up and down.

Punching up pokes fun at a powerful group, which disrupts the current quo.

By mocking a weak or oppressed minority, punching down supports the existing quo.

Humor that is racial, sexist, or crass can be incredibly hurtful.

Making jokes about someone's politics, religion, or other belief systems may also be disrespectful.

Keep the crude, inappropriate jokes to yourself or your buddies who will take anything.

Put-down humor, also known as aggressive humor, uses teasing, sarcasm, and mockery to criticize and control.

This can be amusing when aimed at famous people, but it can be really bad if used against friends and damage friendships.

Trying to See the Positive Side of Things

1. Laugh more often.
A sense of humor is mostly based on laughter. Make it a point to laugh more frequently each day—even at yourself.

Take pleasure in the little things, laugh at the mundane, and find humor in life's calamities.
As often as you can, smile.
Make other folks chuckle as well.
Prioritize laughing for both yourself and other people.

2. Instead of responding, laugh.
Take a step back and chuckle if you ever find yourself in a difficult circumstance.
While anger can be a strong feeling, laughter has a similar hold on our bodies and minds.
Use humor to defuse a situation, crack a joke, or laugh at the circumstance.
You could avoid some anxiety and misery.

Situations that are tense or uncomfortable can benefit from some humor.
People may feel less anxious and more at ease after hearing a joke.

Make a joke when you are about to lash out at someone.

If you and your sister are arguing, you can say, "We've been arguing over this same issue for ten years!
We seem to be stuck as teenagers.

You can say, "I guess you don't look as nice as you did 15 years ago, either," in response to someone making fun of your old car.

3. Give up being defensive.
Let go of everything that makes you feel defensive right away.
Forget about judgments, critiques, and self-doubt.
Instead, keep a sense of humor about them and let those annoying things slide off your back.
Nobody is trying to make fun of you or hurt you.
Instead, chuckle or smile.

4. Be kind to yourself.
One strategy for maintaining your sense of humor is to view oneself with humor.

Everyone must occasionally take themselves seriously, but learning to laugh at oneself is a step toward self-acceptance.

Everyone makes errors because no one is flawless.

Keep a sense of fun and don't take yourself too seriously.

Disregard things you can't change, including your age and attractiveness.

Instead of becoming unhappy if you have a large nose, make fun of yourself.

Be amused by the over-the-hill cards if you're getting older.

Even if it makes you uncomfortable to make fun of yourself, ignore it, especially if you have no control over it.

Laugh at your minor indiscretions and flaws.

Seeing the humor in your humanity is beneficial.

Consider your most embarrassing experiences.

Find an amusing method to relate that story rather than one that is embarrassing.

You'll need to make fun of yourself and possibly embellish or dramatize the circumstances.

5. Allow people some space.
Transferring your sense of humor to others is a crucial aspect of having one.
Try to use the same philosophy to others as you should employ when approaching yourself.
When others make mistakes, be understanding and keep your attention on the good.
Be amused by their errors in the same spirit as you would be on your own.
This can improve your relationship because it makes them feel accepted while also making you feel wonderful.
Glad you're not running an airline," you can say as a joke in place of becoming upset if your employee is constantly late for meetings.

Even if your coworker's joke may have been insulting or of poor taste, you might not need to react negatively.
If you have a sense of humor, you can let things go and decide what to get furious about.

6. Get impulsive.

Most people avoid taking risks because they fear failing or coming off as foolish.

You may overcome these obstacles holding you back by developing a positive sense of humor about yourself.

Regardless of whether your efforts are effective or not, having a sense of humor can help you escape your thoughts and let go of your inhibitions so you can truly live.

Having a sense of humor makes you aware that it's acceptable to appear foolish.

Just make fun of yourself, even if you come across as foolish.

then beam with pride at having been beyond your comfort zone.

Finally, consider the person's personality.

Finding out what they enjoy could make them smile.

Chapter 2

Be mentally prepared

ways to psychologically get ready to accomplish any goal

Every goal we have started as a dream, a wish, or an ambition in our minds.
We fantasize about overcoming obstacles we're unsure we can handle.
We have goals in mind without being 100% convinced we'll ever achieve them, but we wish we could find the time to lead a better or more active lifestyle.

Many people use goal-setting as a realistic method of achieving their objectives and making their aspirations come true.
But not everyone is aware that achieving a goal involves both mental and physical effort.

1. Keep both the big and little picture in mind
You can't just wing it while facing a difficulty!

Many people select how they will train each day after checking the weather when they first get out of bed, but this is not at all productive.

You have the highest chance of success if you have a clear set of objectives and a well-organized plan.

making a range of goals and dividing them into long-term and short-term objectives to maintain motivation.

It's crucial to distinguish between:

Whether we're aiming to swim unassisted, cycle to work every day, or improve our marathon time, outcome objectives are typically what we're after.

Process goals are smaller intermediate targets that will help us increase our strength, stamina, speed, technical skills, or mental toughness. They are the building blocks that lead to our outcome goals.

Consider what objectives you can set as stepping stones to reach your goal if you choose an outcome.

2. Be truthful

Don't lower the bar too much because you might surprise yourself.

On the other hand, if your objective is too ambitious compared to your current capabilities, you risk losing motivation or overtraining to the point of harm.

John Hampshire, a specialist in endurance training, suggests setting an achievable goal and a more challenging stretch goal that you might aim for after reaching the first one.

Hampshire advises his clients to be mindful of the challenges involved in incorporating a fitness program into an already hectic schedule.

Even if you have the physical strength to hit your aim, the demands of your family, job and other responsibilities can make it hard for you to put forth the necessary amount of time and effort.

3. Feel the fear yet go ahead with it.

It makes sense that courage - and audacity - might be one of our greatest qualities, whether it's your first mile or your millionth, as fear is sometimes one of the largest obstacles to achieving our goals.

Andy Waterman, a cyclist, and sports journalist have set himself the lofty goal of finishing his first marathon in 2 hours and 45 minutes.

He admits, "I'm not sure how feasible it is.

But I believe that being ambitious will help me stay motivated for the months I'll be training.

4. Stay faithful to your interests.

Make your objective exciting, according to performance psychologist Dr. Josephine Perry, a rule that holds for both amateur and professional athletes alike.

"What inspires your passion?

That desire will serve as motivation.

What will motivate you to wake up at five in the morning on a chilly, rainy, and windy morning to train?

Additionally, Seear advises her clients to make sure their goals are their own, rather than things they feel they "should" do or accomplish.

It's a lot difficult to persist if you realize that achieving this objective is something you didn't want to achieve in the first place when things get rough, which they always will.

5. Consider your strategy for handling setbacks.

Robbie Britton, who is presently ranked third in the world for 24-hour ultra-marathon running, says that one of his goals is to "go hunting for failures."

"You can't know what you're capable of until you figure out where your limits are," the saying goes.

Even the best-laid training plans can be derailed by unanticipated occurrences like illness, inclement weather, personal tragedies, and injuries.

John Hampshire, an endurance coach, warns that accepting that things won't always go as planned and suggests a degree of flexibility in how you approach your goals.

You'll thank yourself when you cross the finish line if you keep your overarching goal in mind, accept the unavoidable, and get your training back on track.

Chapter 3

Taking Stock of a Situation

It's crucial to look after yourself when something goes wrong at work or with your business.
Important guidance for coping with difficult circumstances.

When situations are bad, focus on the most important person in your life: YOU!

Your business is having problems.
Sales are declining.

For the first time in years, you are experiencing losses.

Several projects are having difficulties.

Your banker wants to meet with you once every month.
He may have only seen you once a year before.

You're wondering if your bonding business truly means to take away all of it when they talk about lowering your line.

The remainder of your organization is feeling disoriented and uninspired because a few important employees have gone.

Some of your finest clients are complaining that business isn't as brisk as it once was.

You worry that no matter what you do, the situation will only worsen.
You're beginning to wonder if this is the last straw.

Unbelievably, many of us have experienced this identical circumstance.

Many people survived, though not everyone.

And there is a lot to learn from the distinction between those who succeeded and those who failed.

My observations have revealed that when business conditions are challenging, successful company executives exhibit a certain trait.

It is not instruction.

It's not a specialty in marketing or finance or anything of the sort.

Instead, something about them personally seems to set them apart.

They took an uncommon action:

THEY CARED ABOUT THEMSELVES!

Surprisingly, they stopped and took care of themselves first before worrying about anything else even though it looked like everything was collapsing around them and there were so many things clamoring for their attention.

Before attempting to make their company in good shape, they first made sure they were in good shape.

Why?
Seek over this list of essential traits to look for in oneself during particularly trying circumstances.
Work on one of these initially if it is lacking or in insufficient quantity.

1. Continue to be confident.
Keeping your composure in a stressful circumstance is the toughest thing to do.
But you have to.
If you don't, your company's other employees will adopt your mindset.
They will begin to panic if you start to.
They will feel as frustrated as you do.

Similar to how you will feel about eventual accomplishment, others will as well.

You'll require talented, dedicated individuals to back your ideas and you.

Don't allow them to believe that you have failed before you even begin.

2. Exchange ideas.

Let's face it, when things are going well, most of us tend to keep our families in the dark.

Simply put, this makes it more challenging to inform people when things are not going well.

However, you owe it to yourself to take that action.

You constantly have to bear a silent weight as the organization's leader.

It can get overwhelming when things are awful. Stop letting it.

Tell your people—at the very least, your important people—what you are confronting because they are also experiencing it.

Furthermore, they undoubtedly have some suggestions on what to do.

They can't assist in solving a problem if they aren't aware that there is one.

3. Pause and reflect.

There are times when it feels like we labor harder but accomplish less.

When things are awful, this might be especially true because your confidence is already under threat.

You're likely juggling more tasks during the day than you ever have before.

Additionally, it appears that you should dedicate extra time to completing all of the necessary tasks.

The issue is that you could not be taking the necessary action.

You might not even understand what must be done.

Stop circling the drain.

Find out which few actions will have the biggest impact.

Determine what you can do with the energy and time you have.

You must pause and reflect for that to occur.

4. Take a nap.

Take some time off. It may seem weird, but this is the best advice in the world.

If you're like the majority of us, you probably put in long hours, work weekends, and take few (if any) vacations.

You must unwind right now.

You won't be able to think if you don't.

You won't be able to address your difficulties if you are unable to think clearly and creatively.

Strange as it may sound, sometimes the finest vacation time is the time you believe you can least afford to take.

Consider this: How often have you encountered a challenge that you simply weren't able to overcome?

Then, after a restless night, in the middle of a TV show, or at another unexpected moment, you suddenly had an epiphany and the solution just came to you.

Your unconscious mind was at work there.

You had a secret computer there.

And it occurred because you stopped overtaxing your circuits by taking the time to rest.

5. Have confidence in yourself.
This can be quite challenging.
We all experience self-doubt from time to time.
But when things are very hard, self-doubt can spiral out of control.

Your success depends on you overcoming this, or, to put it another way, maintaining a robust ego.
The biggest advantage you have in this situation is that your self-confidence and ego are probably already very strong.
You need to have this talent as a core component of your personality to run a business.
So keep in mind and hold onto your self-confidence.

Are you lacking any?
Whether you want them or not, you do, of course.

They include your accountants, bankers, stockholders, workers, family, vendors, friends, and anyone else who has an interest in you or your business.

Their interest could be financial or emotional.

It's a real stake, though.

Everyone who has an interest in something will work to keep it safe.

Amazing things happen when people are engaged.

Do you believe that only huge international corporations are the focus of bankers' delayed-payment schedule calculations?

Do you believe that only employees of competing businesses will pitch in during difficult times?

Our toughest enemy can occasionally be assumptions we make about other people.

You have a team of advisors who will collaborate with you somewhere.

Some may not all be able to solve your difficulties, but they could be able to make a small contribution.

And sometimes, that is all we require.

By now, you've probably seen the common theme - each of these ideas will support keeping your perspective.

You have to do this since you are the company's boss.

You can only ascertain what has to be done if you keep things in perspective.

You can only determine whether you are dealing with a financial crisis, a marketing crisis, an inventory problem, or a mix of all things and more, if you keep your perspective.

You can only ascertain what each component is and how it fits together if you keep your perspective.

You must identify your issues before you can address them.

Before you can do that, you must be able to see the entire forest, not just the trees that are immediately in front of you or the current urgent issue.

You need perspective to be able to achieve it.

Simple to say, challenging to do.

And even if everything must originate from you, make sure you employ others.

They can assist you in creating and maintaining perspective.

So, look after yourself.

You won't be able to handle your problems in a strong, intelligent, or courageous manner unless you do this.

Benefit your company while looking out for your employees.

Chapter 4

Adversity offers valuable insights

When amid a crisis, it can be challenging to envision how the situation will ultimately result in growth.

Research now demonstrates that prior hardship can help you persevere in the face of current stress. Resilience is the capacity to recover from adversity and grow from the challenge.

When compared to both groups who reported a high history of adversity and those who claimed no history of adversity, people who encountered a moderate level of difficulty throughout time reported greater mental health and well-being as well as higher life satisfaction.

You may improve your resilience in the following five ways thanks to past adversity:

They heighten empathy.

There has never been a more crucial time to lead and live with empathy than now.

Empathy is the capacity to understand other people's difficulties and problems from their point of view.

When you feel compelled to intervene in another person's predicament or provide an answer, you may hit an empathy wall.

"Humble curiosity," which is challenging in our hurry-up and get-it-done-now culture, is what activates empathy.

The following phrases encourage "humble curiosity":

They increase self-worth.

Self-efficacy is the conviction that you have that you can succeed despite difficulties and setbacks.

I worked in a program for nearly four years that instructed Army drill sergeants on how to impart resilience training to other troops in their units.

I learned that the training staff had to dance into the plenary room in front of 180 soldiers as a humorous method to illustrate a block of the lesson during my very first training.

Since I move like Elaine from Seinfeld, I had a panic attack just before "the dance" and had to cling to my colleague's arm to keep from passing out.

My brain's response to the workout in the seconds and days that followed was peculiar.

Even though it was a genuinely awful experience, I managed to survive, which inspired my mind to wonder what other difficult obstacles I might be able to overcome.

That is self-efficacy, and there are three distinct ways in which it might grow.

Choose a confidence area or skill or ability that you want to develop first.

Learning through doing is the best technique to advance that talent or skill.

You must practice speaking in front of an audience if you want to become more effective at public speaking.

Learning from others is the second-best method for getting better.

To return to the public speaking example, you may study YouTube videos of outstanding presenters and make notes on their use of humor or storytelling.

And last, getting coaching from a reputable and respected source can help you get better.

Find the people who can provide you with feedback while you pursue your objectives.

They aid in locating the positive.

I've been doing my best to see the positive side of the recent events, but I have to say that most days it's been incredibly challenging.

Though a lot of what's happening feels out of my hands, I've been making an effort to maintain some perspective.

The soldiers I previously mentioned would frequently discuss the advantages of their deployments, including friendships, feeling like they were a part of something greater than themselves and a fresh appreciation for family.

Finding a silver lining in misfortune alters people's coping mechanisms; they seek out social support, express more hope for the future, and have a healthier physiological reaction to stress.

They aid in redefining stress as a problem.

How you approach stress has a huge impact on how you handle it.

While some people can see stress as a threat, others can see it as a challenge.

A challenge response is similar to the fight-or-flight response in that it increases energy, heart rate, and adrenaline, but it differs in a few key areas.

You experience focus instead of fear, a new ratio of stress hormones is released, and it is simpler for you to use your mental and physical resources.

Peak performance, improved concentration, and increased confidence are the outcomes.

Persons who can view stress as a challenge rather than a danger report less despair and anxiety, greater energy, better work performance, and higher levels of life satisfaction.

You can use the following queries to train your challenge response:

Where in the circumstance do I have power, influence, or leverage?

What precise course of action may I take?

What do I do well?

What assets do I possess?

What gives me the confidence to know I can manage this?

Even if it doesn't feel that way right now, even if your world feels out of control and your stress levels are at an all-time high, remember that previous challenges, no matter how tiny, have given you some ability to handle this one.
Resilience isn't always attractive; on some days, it merely involves getting by as best you can.
What you're doing right now is sufficient.

Chapter 5

Have a purpose

What is the Meaning and Purpose of Life?

Living a meaningful life requires having a feeling of purpose.

It is the source of all passion and has the power to uplift us to higher planes of lasting enjoyment while fostering fortitude in the face of enormous adversity.

We frequently talk about needing, seeking, or having a feeling of purpose, but in our world of continuing life projects, many occupations, and a very flexible economy, it can be difficult to find.

So what exactly does "purpose" mean?

The word "purpose" has its origins in the Anglo-French word "purpose," which denotes an intention, aim, or goal.

Therefore, the purpose is goal-oriented action; broadly speaking, it might relate to intentionally putting the toilet seat down, intentionally taking care of your loved ones, or intentionally getting wasted on the weekend.

We will need to hone the notion before discussing the particular kind of purpose to which I alluded in the introduction.

However, we must first determine the function of purpose in a person's life before we can further develop the idea.

This entails determining the goal of one's life.

In other words, the ultimate end, the end of all other ends, or the goal of all other objectives is the meaning of life.

This simply translates to the question, "Why do we do what we do?" in everyday English.

Fortunately, Aristotle is a useful resource that can be applied to resolve this specific kind of philosophical entanglement.

According to Aristotle, happiness is the ultimate end, meaning that all other objectives are geared toward achieving happiness.

As a result, happiness is the goal of life.

However, before going any further, it's important to understand what Aristotle means by happiness.

Aristotle distinguished happiness from hedonistic temporary pleasures by defining it as "eudemonia," which is Greek for "good spirit" or "living well."

According to Aristotle, leading a good life entails acting morally and sensibly, according to his ethics of moderation as outlined in the Nicomachean Ethics.

To sum up the conceptual development to date, we may state that the goal of life purpose is to guide one toward leading a morally upright life.

Because it serves as an overarching meta-purpose, a sense of purpose in life is different from the sense of purpose one experiences while performing regular goal-oriented activities like going grocery shopping.

This indicates that it is a purpose that molds all other purposes to be in line with a good notion.
For instance, if one's life purpose is greatly influenced by a dedication to the well-being of one's children, this overarching objective may impact one's goals while grocery shopping, regulating the types of foods one chooses to purchase.

Thus, the regulative nature of life aims.
It restrains our fleeting impulses and hedonistic goals to direct our behavior toward an ideal.
Recall that I said earlier that the goal of finding one's life purpose is to guide one toward an ideal of a good life.
I went on to prove that having a life purpose has a regulating effect.

Life-purpose can sometimes be referred to as "moral purpose" because it serves to regulate moral behavior.

Character is what shows a person's moral purpose and the types of things he picks or shuns.

In Aristotle's virtue ethics, personal willpower plays a significant role in character growth.

How to Develop a Purposeful Mindset

Find your passion, we are constantly told in today's society.

This, in my opinion, is very poor counsel.

It's the same as advising a person who is miserable to just "find happiness."

If you're looking for your passion in a purposeless fog, you're probably going to bumble around in a confused fog, frustrated.

Many demographics, such as the elderly, retirees, veterans, former elite athletes, fresh graduates, or people going through a midlife crisis, struggle with a lack of purpose.

This issue was referred to by Erikson as the identity struggle or role confusion that occurs during adolescence.

In contrast to Erikson, I would contend that this is a problem that affects people of all ages and is not only a teenage problem.

Because our social positions have an impact on how we feel about ourselves, every significant change in our lives might result in an identity crisis that undermines our feeling of purpose.

What then is the remedy for aimlessness?

It appears simple in theory.

Finding someone in need of assistance is not difficult.

The issue is that if you aren't first valuable to yourself, how can you be beneficial to anyone else?

So here is the first step:

Put yourself to use.

Attend to your essential requirements.

Organize the chaos in your daily life and the clutter in your physical environment.

Give sleep, diet, and exercise a priority.

Start small if all of this seems overwhelming.

More than just your room has to be cleaned when you clean your room.

The first step to getting yourself back on track amid your lack of purpose is to take care of yourself.

You might start to see farther than yourself as the fog starts to clear.

Next comes step two:

Be of service to your loved ones or close pals.

You can be valuable to those near you if you've been sufficiently beneficial to yourself and can assist from a place of sincere giving.

I bring up "genuine giving" because a lot of individuals strive to help others without first taking care of their own needs.

This frequently leads to codependent relationships when you fill your self-esteem gap by taking care of others.

We continuously feel the need to validate ourselves in front of others because we are dealing with poisonous shame.

The next step is this: Once you have resolved these inner conflicts and can interact in close, meaningful connections with others,

Be of service to society at large.

Once you've taken care of your own needs and can help people who are near you, you can help society as a whole.

This could occur in several ways.

You can contribute to some kind of social change through your work, volunteer work, leisure pursuits, or even as an activist.

The most important thing is that your method of contribution plays to your particular abilities.

A lack of congruence between your strengths, values, and interests can limit how valuable you are in the work and how motivated you will feel as a result.

Knowing and developing your strengths is necessary before you can find harmony between your skills and your role.

Chapter 6

Embrace adversity as a chance for opportunity

11 Ways To Turn Adversity Into Opportunity

Many of us seem to have learned from 2020 that hardships are unavoidable and that some people can thrive under difficult circumstances while others find it difficult to get out of bed in the morning.

Genuinely resilient people discover methods to turn adversity into an opportunity rather than just navigating the rough waters.

They consider it as a necessary fuel for the journey of life.

That is not to argue that those who are strong do not feel the same things when tragedy hits.

To pain is to be human.

But those with greater mental toughness take stock of the situation, weigh their choices swiftly, make plans, and firmly commit to a course of action.

Instead of spending time and exhausting your emotions by wallowing in sadness.

Read on if you're looking for a few life hacks or even just some easy reminders for how to turn hardship into opportunity.

1. Embrace it.
The first and most effective approach to start surviving any life ambush is to accept your current situation rather than trying to hide from it or go back to the safety of your comfort zone.
When life severely beats you down, identify the cause, take responsibility for it, and lean in.
Your fighting strategy starts with this.

2. Develop compassion for oneself.
We all go through challenging periods in our life.
But when we are in pain, we frequently fail to have compassion for ourselves.
Once you've accepted it, the next step to overcoming adversity more quickly is to practice more self-compassion.

By doing this, you will enhance your emotional health and give yourself the courage to overcome obstacles and continue on your path.

3. Control your feelings.
Maintaining self-discipline requires emotional intelligence.
If you don't control your emotions, they will control you.
Starting to feel your emotions physically is the best method to start controlling your emotions.
When anything or someone triggers you, pay attention to what happens and mentally record the emotions that arise.
Self-awareness and acknowledging your feelings are powerful strategies for reducing the power of your emotions.

4. Use comedy as a tool.
It's possible to reframe your situation's story by laughing in the face of difficulty.
Of course, depending on the seriousness of the situation, this might not be a viable or appropriate option.

It's not about discounting your sorrow.

Instead, it's about relying on uplifting feelings when you most need them.

According to studies, having a positive outlook on life and facing challenges head-on makes you more adaptable in your thinking and problem-solving.

5. Take part in healthy activities.

Stress reduction and mental clarity are aided by mental and physical wellness practices like meditation, exercise, and a clean diet.

When our minds are clear, we make better choices that are more grounded in logic than in unfavorable feelings.

Additionally, it's beneficial for you!

6. Get rid of the clutter.

Adversity also gives us fantastic chances to get rid of the things that are cluttering up our lives, such worthless endeavors unrelated to our values and goals, ridiculous things we believe we adore, things we squander money on, and even individuals who aren't looking out for us.

7. Be grateful .

Have you received a curveball from life?

Good!

Make the most of the chance to learn and develop.

By expressing thankfulness for your challenges, you reduce their impact and change your mindset, transitioning from "why me?" analysis paralysis to goal-oriented action.

8. Establish a growth attitude.

Those with a growth attitude are capable of overcoming obstacles with grace.

They decide to adopt a winning mentality.

They don't think their IQ is predetermined.

Instead, they welcome challenges, keep going despite losses, view effort as the key to mastery, and take feedback to heart.

Any form of adversity can be incredibly challenging to overcome.

Nobody wants to go through difficult times in life.

But you wouldn't comprehend tranquility if you had never felt agony.

9. Hold fast to your goal.
Or look for another.
Passion and purpose are essential tools for life's fight.
They strengthen the required emotional connection to objectives and intended results.
The wind might be taken out of your sails when events occur that are out of your control.
But you'll always find a way to move forward if you're working toward something that means something to you.

10. Continue to have faith in your ability.
People who overcome adversity start by having confidence in their ability to move forward.
It is doubtful that you will succeed if you feel helpless and powerless.
If you're willing to use your strengths—or perhaps even learn new ones—you'll be able to overcome this issue and many more in the future.

11. Reflect and move on.

Reflecting and staying are very different things.

Reflection is an intentional process.

It serves a function.

When hardship hits, take the following actions:

Accept your reality, assess your resources and dangers, use whatever lessons you may have learned from past mistakes, create an action plan, choose a course of action, and go on with conviction.

Chapter 7

Don't to give up

Real achievement requires suffering, overcoming difficulties, overcoming setbacks, and persevering in the face of several failures.
The wealthiest individuals of today have demonstrated to us how tenacity and self-confidence can propel us to extraordinary success.
Never should we adopt an "I give up" mentality.

What Takes Place When You Adopt a Never-Give-Up Attitude?

When we choose to persevere on our path to success, there are benefits we can reap.
Here are several justifications for having a never-give-up mentality.

1 Your fears will be gone.
Your endurance and efforts will be defined by significant events like a work promotion,

graduation, a new home, relationships, and conquering hardships.

All of these are the outcomes of your decision to keep working toward your goals rather than giving up.

The ability to never give up can be used to eliminate doubts and pessimistic thoughts, empowering you to face any challenge.

Realizing all you had to go through and the hardships you had overcome to achieve your goals made your success all the more wonderful.

It's all about the mindset that helps to start a war. The key is how you fight on with the conviction that you will prevail in life.

2. You'll have access to new creative opportunities.

Some of us were brought up in our culture with the conviction that we should follow social norms.

As a result, our attitude is also permitted with some limitations.

We then start to live with constrained abilities and aspirations instead of considering how to be inventive and bountiful.

When we adopt a never-give-up mentality, we begin to recognize the true value of our lives and dare ourselves to try anything.

We discover our skills and demonstrate our capacity to make things that are better for ourselves and the entire society.

We start learning the value of creativity and how having a creative mindset may lead to better possibilities and novel viewpoints on life.

3. You dare to try things that others might be frightened of.

You will learn how to put effort into all aspects of life when you decide never to give up, whether it be in sports, hobbies, physical health, or general well-being.

You will be inspired to strive for more noteworthy outcomes of your actions toward your dreams as a result.

You'll take chances by doing activities that other people would find terrifying.

As a result, you stand out from the competition. Your attitude will be one of high spirits and opportunity hunger.
You decide to focus on being strong rather than on your weak attitudes.

4 You'll feel a spark of desire.
What motivates us to dream and begin living our lives?
We aspire to accomplish goals and transform into the people we've always imagined.
All success begins with a desire, not a hope or a wish, but a strong, transcendental desire that pulses with intensity.

Nowadays, a typical issue for some people is a lack of desire and motivation to push oneself toward difficult but successful pathways.
We require constant igniting of our desires.
We all desire to realize and accomplish our aspirations and goals.

We should keep moving and keep ourselves motivated – from start to finish.

5. You now have a higher emotional quotient.
Your emotional IQ is a significant factor in making things work out well.
It is the capacity to recognize, communicate, and regulate your emotions.
Even when we offer everything we have, there are instances when our plans to accomplish our goals fall short of our expectations.

We err, and we might err again.
It's okay if we occasionally fail.
Consider this situation as a typical step in any process.
What matters is how you deal with such a setback and how you decide to apply the lessons you've learned.
You can limit the harm and improve your efficiency in a variety of scenarios when you can manage your emotions in those situations.

6. You'll think that anything is conceivable that you can perceive.

The benefit of having a positive outlook on life is having the drive to motivate yourself to take action.

When you are confident in your abilities, you can overcome obstacles that may otherwise prevent you from succeeding.

Success is frequently determined by your perception and your willingness to step outside of your comfort zone.

You have the power to act.

Of course, there is only one way to overcome that: never give up.

7. You learn to be ready for everything.

We must keep in mind that we must mentally prepare for failure in any endeavor we undertake.

You won't be willing to take risks because you're terrified of what other people would think.

Be fearless.

The more prepared you are for everything, the stronger you get and the more determined you are to pursue your goals.

Because, on the other hand, if you quit while you are struggling, you will not succeed.

8. You establish strong work ethics.

Your defense against failures will be your commitment to do whatever it takes to achieve your goals.

As a result, you are more driven to persevere and give your work more meaning.

You will accept the idea that there is always a way to accomplish goals.

You learn how to give the most important tasks top priority.

9. Never Giving Up Will Make You Happy, Rule.

When we succeed, we experience deep joy because all of our efforts have been successful.

We rejoice since we overcame all the challenging obstacles.

We can appreciate life more when we choose to persevere since happiness can be found in both achievement and contentment.

10. You Acquire New Knowledge.

When we persist and choose not to give up, we learn a lot.

We can discover that we each have untapped strengths and potential.

We acquire the ability to maintain our motivation.

More significantly, we decide to keep trying and we discover how to successfully turn our failures into successes.

We develop as role models for others and acquire the capacity to accomplish more in the future.

Keep in mind that as you go along your path to success, it may become more difficult to carry out your plans and dreams.

During the voyage, you can lose your motivation and drive, and you might consider giving up early.

What you should do is reflect on the rationale for your initial decision to start it.

Who stands to gain from this?

What does it mean to you, and why should you do it?

You just need to believe that the reason you started and the importance of what you are doing will drive you to persevere.

Chapter 8

Keep a positive mindset

9 Ways To Authentically Foster Positive Thoughts

1. Be grateful to everyone!
Appreciate your father for bringing you on vacation and your mother for cooking your favorite meal.
Thank your friend for all of his assistance.
Send your sister a heartfelt congratulations on passing her exams along with a small gift.
Thank the waitstaff and bus drivers for their assistance.
You'll be amazed at the benefits of adopting this constructive thought pattern for your life if you do!
When you express your thanks to someone you meet, you immediately feel satisfied and happy inside, which spreads to other people.

2. Everyone errs occasionally.

Thus, let's now practice accepting and forgiving them.

Please refrain from yelling at anyone who makes a mistake.

Consider the person's positive traits instead.

Even better, offer to assist the person in any manner you can.

Keep in mind that we have all made a lot of blunders in life.

And our relatives, friends, parents, and coworkers have all readily pardoned us.

So let's adopt this constructive mental attitude and develop the ability to tolerate and forgive others.

You might even offer a prayer for the person to recover from their error.

3. Display a "No Entry" sign to our "Tit for Tat" mentality

Our "wrong intellect" is the cause of our negativity.

Furthermore, because of its nature, it quickly grows and develops into a significant barrier.

When this happens, people start to send us bad energy, which we subsequently return to them.

We would reply, "You are a sick, paranoid person," if our friend said, "You are a lazy bone."

What did it help us achieve?

This is an endless cycle of "Tit for Tat."

Only positivity can break this pattern.

Decide to adopt a positive mind pattern going forward.

Never utter anything hurtful or unkind to anyone.

Instead, wherever feasible, focus on their positive traits.

In contrast, negativity will bind terrible karmas, which you will have to suffer in the next life, whereas this promotes inner calm.

4. Permit your house to continue to be a lovely garden.

Each house has several distinct characters that blend.

Since they are all members of the same family, these personalities must get along peacefully.

One might need to make adjustments and let go of some things.

But the most crucial thing is to embrace all of nature's diversity.

There are many different kinds of plants and flowers in a lovely garden, including cacti, hibiscus, daffodils, and roses.

Don't they all coexist peacefully with one another?

Tiny thorns are found on roses.

Who will lose if you complain about the thorns?

But if you figure out how to pluck the rose while avoiding the thorns, you succeed!

So, always think positively; don't allow the rose to wither because of the thorns, and don't forget to appreciate the thorns as well!

5. Examine an uplifting book.

Negativity spreads quickly.

If there is negativity all around you, you might soon start to feel that way.

Therefore, be courageous and disengage from the unfavorable environment if you want to end this cycle.

Make a deliberate decision to live your life without sadness, anguish, resentment, negativity, or sorrow.

Adopt positive thinking instead.

6. See noble, do noble"

Allow it to inspire you when you witness someone with a noble character who freely gives away his possessions to others for their enjoyment.

You will soon find yourself on the road to optimism if you keep an eye out for the noble qualities in others.

7. Count your possessions!

Peace comes from positivity, whereas suffering only comes from negativity.

This is the rationale for the Lord's advice to focus on what we do have rather than shed tears over what we lack.

Adopting this constructive mental attitude will enable you to see the bright side of any circumstance.

8. Exercise perseverance and patience

Read accounts of famous saints who showed tremendous forbearance and patience before ultimately defeating the evil powers with their love and goodness.

These real-life examples encourage us to adopt the same constructive thinking habits and advance in our personal growth.

9. Keep your heart pure and upbeat while attempting to maintain smooth interactions outside.

We refrain from speaking badly a lot because we don't want to argue or confront the other person.

But within, our thought pattern is profoundly negative.

We continue to be irritated by them and grow to detest them.

It's not good at all!
When your internal vibrations are off, all of your external efforts are in vain.
Create a clear inner intention by telling yourself, "I don't want to have any disagreement with anyone, not even in my thoughts.
I agree wholeheartedly with everything he or she says, both within and outside.
Decide with absolute certainty that "I only wish to follow good thought patterns."

Chapter 9

Believe in your capabilities

We might be our own biggest supporters or our own biggest detractors.
And it matters how the two possibilities differ from one another.
Success depends on your ability to believe in yourself.
Your ability to believe in yourself, or self-efficacy, can help you achieve your goals.

Higher self-efficacy has been linked to success in areas like academic achievement or quitting smoking, according to studies.
You can accomplish anything if you have faith.
A growth mentality and the capacity to accept and learn from your failures should be developed.
These qualities can require some patience and time to develop.

The advantages of self-confidence

The secret to both personal and professional success is self-belief.

When you err, do you criticize yourself?
Do you believe that speaking negatively to yourself will improve you in some way?

One thing is to make mistakes.
But eventually, you have to accept your mistakes and move on.
Otherwise, you will just be held back by that energy.
You won't be able to take chances or do what's necessary to advance toward your objectives.
You must ultimately have confidence in yourself.
You'll be one step closer to creating a better life if you do this.

Here are some reasons to trust your judgment and your instincts:

1. If not you, then who will?

It's wonderful if you have a network of individuals that care about and support you.

But at the end of the day, only you can act on the opportunities in your life.

You will eventually need to make a leap of faith in your life.

You'll need to have faith in your capacity for survival.

2. You'll handle failure better.

Look, we've all experienced it.

Even the most successful people have experienced failure.

However, they are aware that growth will continue as long as they continue to study.

You just need to have faith in yourself to be like that.

3. Being comes after doing (sometimes you have to act positive to get positive)

People don't value you if you don't think you're deserving of them.

To act as though you believe in yourself, you must first suspend disbelief.

Both you and others will view the world and yourself with fresh perspectives.

Negativity feeds on itself.

You should change the script because of this.

More positive people will come into your life as a result of your increased positive behavior.

4. You'll motivate yourself to continue.

You'll confront all sorts of problems in life.

You'll be worn out, on guard, and ready to give up.

But if you have confidence in yourself, you'll reflect on all your past accomplishments and keep in mind that you can do even better.

5. You'll begin achieving your objectives.

If you don't even believe you can accomplish your goals, how can you?

Success shouldn't come as a surprise to you; rather, it should serve as confirmation of your self-confidence.

Being confident in oneself improves concentration and productivity.

Since optimism is contagious, it will spread and encourage others to have confidence in themselves.

When you believe in yourself, magic happens.
It's your potential, not magic, of course.
And you don't have to go through the process of changing to a more optimistic growth mindset alone; BetterUp coaches are here for just this purpose.
We want to assist you in reaching your full potential because you matter.

Three common obstacles to confidence are as follows:

1. Comparative
The key is perception.
Even if you may not be doing well, you may see someone else succeeding.
Keep in mind that people only allow you to view certain things on social media, and they often don't promote their troubles.

It's like the proverb that reads, "Don't judge a book by its cover."

Additionally, there is space for you and your peers to prosper.
Feel happy for your successful friends and coworkers without becoming envious.

2. The past
The adage "the past can haunt you" has some basis in reality.
A difficult childhood or an unpleasant relationship is difficult to overcome.
Self-analysis is beneficial, but not at the cost of your mental well-being.
An excellent method to go through your previous issues and prevent them from impacting your present is to speak with a mental health specialist.

3. Present connections
Do you have a friend who constantly criticizes you?

Perhaps you dread seeing a parent or a coworker because they make you feel inferior.

Humans are by nature social creatures, but not getting someone's approval can be damaging to your self-esteem.

How to get around obstacles

Roadblocks are temporary hurdles that can always be overcome, so keep that in mind.

Try the following tactics:

Positive thinking: Much of who you are and what you do comes from your thoughts.

To overcome whatever challenges you face, you must have faith in your capacity to overcome it.

Visualizing your desired outcome will help you stay motivated even when circumstances seem hopeless and self-doubt creeps in.

Although the past cannot be changed, the future can be improved.

Whatever you desire to do is doable.

Make a move:
Although thinking and "talking the talk" is crucial, you must eventually "walk the walk."
As you advance and reap the benefits of your efforts to effect change, you'll feel better about yourself and your abilities.

Seven techniques to help you have confidence in yourself

Don't let the challenges deter you.
Seven changes you can make to feel better about yourself are listed below:

1. Establish wholesome practices
Love for oneself depends on living well.
It's crucial to fuel your body with nutritious food and liquids, exercise, sleep, and take breaks during your workday.
You'll feel less anxious and have more energy to face each day.
Keeping a balance and taking all the necessary steps to prepare yourself for success are key components of self-love.

2. Surround yourself with positive individuals
The self-help expert Tony Robbins asserts that "proximity is power."
That statement is true.
Your perspective and motivation are influenced by the company you keep.
Seek out those that encourage you to be your best selves and those who can assist you in doing so.
People that are encouraging will challenge you and keep you going when times are tough.

Keep an eye out for individuals who exhibit these negative personality qualities.
Spend less time with people who make you feel exhausted, down, or full of self-doubt.
Cut them out of your life.
If that's not possible, try to spend as little time as possible with each other.

3. Give your thoughts on food
The law of attraction holds some truth in that both positive and negative energy that you put

out into the world will eventually come back to you.

Your mindset indeed affects how you interact with the outside world and how other people interact with you, even though this may not be a natural law.

How you view yourself and the world has a lot to do with what you feed your mind.

Find media that uplifts and inspires you, whether it be through books, movies, or social media.

Your brain will gradually change its thinking patterns if you frequently read encouraging and uplifting content.

Spend as little time as possible with negative or cynical viewpoints.

Cynicism undermines your belief in other people, kills your motivation, and removes your optimism for the future, even though it's vital to be realistic and accept the ups and downs of life.

It also doesn't improve how you feel about yourself.

4. Don't let fear hold you back.

Insecurity is common.
That cannot be a hindrance to you.
Speak up.
Set objectives.
Your brain produces dopamine when you learn something new or overcome a challenge, which makes you feel better physically with each step you take.
When mistakes happen, try to keep in mind that you may learn from them rather than feeling tiny or disappointed.
That is to say, failures can spur growth.

5. Make use of your inner fortitude
Sometimes all you can do is push through.
You are not a failure just because you struggled to complete a task.
Find your grit, and persevere despite the obstacles.

6. Recognize your successes
Celebrate both little and significant achievements.
Honor your interests.

Choose to engage in self-compassion instead of self-criticism.

7. Work on your strengths
It's common to concentrate on your weaknesses when you're depressed.
Work on identifying your advantages instead.
Requesting input from others might be beneficial.
Then, concentrate on improving those abilities; it will make you feel more capable.

ISBN 9798353312895

Elements of Linear and Multilinear Algebra

John M. Erdman